Fish Community Monitoring at George Washington Carver National Monument

2006, 2007 and 2010 Status Report

Natural Resource Data Series NPS/HTLN/NRDS—2011/138

Hope R. Dodd

National Park Service
Heartland I&M Network
Wilson's Creek National Battlefield
6424 W Farm Road 182
Republic, MO 65738

David E. Bowles

National Park Service
Heartland I&M Network
Wilson's Creek National Battlefield
6424 W Farm Road 182
Republic, MO 65738

Samantha K. Mueller

University of Minnesota Duluth
Biology
207 SSB
1035 Kirby Drive
Duluth, MN 55812

Myranda K. Clark

Missouri State University
Biology Department
901 S. National Avenue
Springfield, MO 65897

February 2011

U.S. Department of the Interior
National Park Service
Natural Resource Program Center
Fort Collins, Colorado

The National Park Service, Natural Resource Program Center publishes a range of reports that address natural resource topics of interest and applicability to a broad audience in the National Park Service and others in natural resource management, including scientists, conservation and environmental constituencies, and the public.

The Natural Resource Data Series is intended for the timely release of basic data sets and data summaries. Care has been taken to assure accuracy of raw data values, but a thorough analysis and interpretation of the data has not been completed. Consequently, the initial analyses of data in this report are provisional and subject to change.

All manuscripts in the series receive the appropriate level of peer review to ensure that the information is scientifically credible, technically accurate, appropriately written for the intended audience, and designed and published in a professional manner.

This report received informal peer review by subject-matter experts who were not directly involved in the collection, analysis, or reporting of the data. Data in this report were collected and analyzed using methods based on established, peer-reviewed protocols and were analyzed and interpreted within the guidelines of the protocols.

Views, statements, findings, conclusions, recommendations, and data in this report do not necessarily reflect views and policies of the National Park Service, U.S. Department of the Interior. Mention of trade names or commercial products does not constitute endorsement or recommendation for use by the U.S. Government.

This report is available from the Heartland Inventory & Monitoring website (http://science.nature.nps.gov/im/units/HTLN/) and the Natural Resource Publications Management website (http://www.nature.nps.gov/publications/NRPM).

Please cite this publication as:

NPS 920/106747, February 2011

Contents

Figures

Tables

Abstract

George Washington Carver National Monument (GWCA), located in southwest Missouri, was established to interpret the historic and cultural resources related to the birthplace, childhood, and achievements of George Washington Carver. Part of interpreting this historic site is the natural history that surrounds the events of Carver's early life and the maintenance and protection of these natural resources (National Park Service, 1999). The watersheds of streams within GWCA are predominately agricultural and rural residential land use. Many native fish populations in the Midwest have been adversely impacted throughout their ranges by a number of factors associated with land use changes, including habitat loss and fragmentation, sedimentation, and reduced water quality. Although human induced disturbance can dramatically alter aquatic systems, GWCA may offer important habitat and protection for native fish species.

Beginning in 2006, fish communities, water quality, and physical habitat were sampled at three streams in the park to determine the status and long-term trends in fish community composition and to correlate this community data to water quality and habitat conditions. In general, the fish communities within GWCA were found to be diverse and healthy. Numerous native fish species were present in these streams and community composition consisted of several darter, sculpin, and madtom species that are sensitive to poor water quality and habitat conditions. Low occurrence of fish anomalies or diseases and high biotic integrity scores suggest that the fish populations are healthy and that streams within the park are in good condition.

Acknowledgments

We would like to thank staff at George Washington Carver National Monument, Tyler Cribbs and Jan Hinsey from Heartland I&M Network, Jake Waters from Missouri State University, and Shawn Hodges from Buffalo National River for assistance with field work. Also, thanks to Jen Haack (Heartland I&M Network) for GPS/GIS assistance.

Introduction

George Washington Carver National Monument (GWCA), located in the Ozark Highlands of southwest Missouri, was established to interpret the historic and cultural resources related to the birthplace, childhood, and achievements of George Washington Carver. A part of interpreting this historic site is the natural history that surrounds the events of Carver's early life and the maintenance and protection of these natural resources (National Park Service, 1999). GWCA is approximately 0.85 km^2 with 0.59 km^2 of restored prairie and approximately 1.8 km of streams. The watersheds of the streams within GWCA are predominately agricultural and rural residential land use. Many native fish populations have been adversely impacted throughout their ranges by a number of factors associated with land use changes, including habitat loss and fragmentation, sedimentation, and reduced water quality. As a result of degraded stream conditions in the Midwest, the Arkansas darter (*Etheostoma cragini*), a native stream fish found at GWCA, has become a candidate species for listing under the Endangered Species Act of 1973 (63 FR 69008). This species is now found only in tributaries of the Arkansas River basin (Pflieger 1997). Although anthropogenic disturbances at the watershed scale can dramatically alter a lotic system, protecting portions of Ozark streams on publicly owned lands may offer protection for native species.

Fish communities are an important component of Ozark stream systems. Because changes or shifts in stream habitat complexity and water quality often determine biotic communities, including fish (Lazorchak *et al.* 1998), monitoring trends in fish community composition along with associated habitat conditions serves as a strong basis for measuring stream integrity. Many fish species are considered intolerant of habitat alterations and monitoring their assemblages can serve as a useful tool to assess changes in water and habitat quality (Karr 1981; Robison and Buchanan 1988; Pflieger 1997; Barbour *et al.* 1999; Peitz 2005). Accordingly, trends in the composition and abundance of fish populations historically have been used to assess the biological integrity of streams (Karr 1981; Barbour *et al.* 1999; Moulton *et al.* 2002). Moreover, the intrinsic value of fish to the public as environmental indicators and as a recreational opportunity makes the status of fish diversity a valuable interpretive topic for the park visitor and an informative tool for protecting and conserving the aquatic resources at GWCA.

Objectives of fish community monitoring at GWCA are: (1) to determine the status and long term trends in fish richness, diversity, abundance, and community composition and (2) to correlate the long-term community data to overall water quality and habitat condition.

Methods

Details on methods of site selection, fish sampling, and habitat and water quality data collection not listed in this report can be found in the Protocol for Monitoring Fish Communities in Small Streams in the Heartland Inventory and Monitoring Network (Dodd *et al.* 2008).

Study Area and Site Selection

Portions of three wadeable streams run through GWCA: Carver Branch (~ 1.0 km), Williams Branch (~0.25 km), and Harkins Branch (~ 0.51km). A reach was selected at the downstream end of each stream near the park boundary or just upstream of the confluence for tributaries that flow into larger streams within the park (Figure 1). Reach length was defined as 20 times the mean wetted stream width (MWSW) with a minimum of 150 m, allowing inclusion of representative channel units (riffle, run, and pool habitats) located within the stream (Moulton *et al.*, 2002). Because the streams at GWCA were small and narrow, the minimum reach length of 150 m was sampled for each stream.

Fish Collection

Fish communities were sampled in May/June of 2006-2007 and 2010. Fish were collected using a single pass with a pulsed DC backpack electrofishing unit throughout each sampling reach. During sampling, fish were collected with nets and placed in aerated buckets. All fish were identified to species, if possible, and counted. A subsample of 30 individuals per species were measured and weighed, and any anomalies (deformities, eroded fins, lesions, tumors, and blackspot parasite) were recorded. Fish that were too small or that were difficult to identify in the field were preserved for laboratory identification. All other fish were released back into the sample reach. Details on fish collection and sample processing techniques can be found in Dodd *et al.* (2008) (SOP #4).

Habitat and Water Quality

Physical habitat and water quality data were collected in conjunction with fish sampling. An 11 transect method was used to collect data on general channel morphology, fish cover, and bank conditions within the entire reach. In-stream habitat (depth, velocity, substrate, *etc.*) and fish cover (presence of boulders, hydrophytes, *etc.*) were assessed at three points per transect (see Dodd *et al.* (2008), SOP #5 for a list of all habitat parameters collected). Fish cover along the banks (undercut banks, overhanging terrestrial vegetation, *etc.*) and bank/riparian stability were assessed on the left and right banks at each transect. Hourly CORE 5 water quality data (temperature, dissolved oxygen, pH, specific conductance, and turbidity) was collected using loggers deployed downstream of the reach for at least 24 hours. Detailed methods on habitat and water quality collection are located in Dodd *et al.* (2008).

Data Analysis

Biological metrics were calculated for each reach sampled in 2006-2007 and 2010. These metrics reflect fish community diversity (species richness and Simpson's Diversity Index), abundance (catch per unit effort), composition (number and percent composition of sensitive taxa), and overall stream integrity (Index of Biotic Integrity). Community diversity was assessed using Simpson's Diversity Index which gives the probability that two individuals picked at random from the site are the same species. Therefore, the index decreases with increasing diversity and ranges from 0 (completely diverse) to 1 (no diversity). For community composition, number and percent composition of sucker (Catastomidae), sunfish (Centrarchidae), and darter/sculpin/madtom (*Etheostoma* and *Percina/Cottus/Noturus*) species were calculated because these metrics are typically used in several Index of Biotic Integrity (IBI) calculations (Karr 1981, Dauwalter *et al.* 2003, Smogor 2005) and demonstrate sensitivity to human disturbance. The IBI developed by Dauwalter *et al.* (2003) was used to assess overall stream health and includes seven metrics: 1) percent of individuals as algivorous/herbivorous, invertivorous, and piscivorous; 2) percent with an anomaly (disease, eroded fins, lesions, or tumors) or blackspot parasite; 3) percent as green sunfish (*Lepomis cyanellus*), bluegill (*Lepomis macrochirus*), yellow bullhead (*Ameiurus natalis*), or channel catfish (*Ictalurus punctatus*); 4) percent invertivores; 5) percent top carnivores; 6) number of darter/sculpin/madtom species; 7) number of lithophilic (sand/gravel) spawning species. Each of the seven raw metric values was scored from 0 to 10 based on upper and lower thresholds developed for the Ozarks region. The metric scores were added to calculate an IBI score that ranges from 0 to 100. Based on this IBI score, the overall integrity of the stream is classified from very poor to excellent: very poor = 0-20; poor = 20-40; fair = 40-60; good = 60-80; excellent (reference condition) = 80-100. More detailed methods on calculating biological metrics used in this report can be found in Dauwalter *et al.* (2003).

Physical habitat and water quality data were summarized using averages with standard errors (SE) or percentages, where appropriate. Physical habitat data were analyzed as in-stream habitat, fish cover, and bank stability. Analysis of in-stream substrate data used the Wentworth code for particle sizes (see SOP #5 in Dodd *et al.* 2008 for the code categories and size ranges). For assessment of stream banks, categories of bank angle, percent vegetation, height, and substrate were used to assess overall bank stability. Water quality data were analyzed using averages and standard errors.

Figure 1. Reach locations for long-term fish monitoring at GWCA.

Results

Fish Community

Species richness (i.e., number of species) ranged from 9 to 13 in 2006, 5 to 12 in 2007, and 9 to 15 in 2010 (Figure 2, top panel). In each year, Harkins Branch had the highest number of species. Richness was highest for Carver Branch and Harkins Branch in 2010 and lowest for Williams Branch in 2007. Simpson's Diversity Index ranged from 0.41 to 0.97 at Carver Creek, 0.21 to 0.47 at Williams Branch, and 0.15 to 0.38 at Harkins Branch (Figure 2, middle panel). Diversity was highest at Harkins Branch (i.e., low Simpson's Index) and lowest at Carver Branch (i.e., high Simpson's Index) in 2007 and 2010. Carver Branch showed the greatest variability in diversity across years. Fish abundance ranged from 7 to 18 fish/min at Carver Branch, 2 to 3 fish/min at Williams Branch, and 3 to 25 fish/min at Harkins Branch (Figure 2, bottom panel). Harkins Branch had the highest variability in abundance due to high numbers of Stoneroller spp. (*Campostoma spp.*) in 2006, while Williams Branch had the lowest variability (difference of 1 fish/min) among years. At all sites, abundance was lowest in 2007.

All streams had low numbers and composition of sucker and sunfish species with Harkins Branch having the highest composition of sunfish compared to the other streams (Table 1). Community composition of darter/sculpin/madtom species (species sensitive to siltation and poor water quality) was highest at Williams Branch, although the number of darter/sculpin/madtom species was low (2 species) in 2007. Arkansas darters were found in all three streams, but in low numbers (Appendix 1). IBI scores ranged from 55 to 68 at Carver Branch, 65 to 81 at Williams Branch, and 52 to 73 at Harkins Branch (Table 2). All reaches rated as "good" in 2006 and 2007. Both Carver Branch and Harkins Branch rated as "fair" in 2010 due to more occurrences of anomalies in both streams and the higher percentage of tolerant green sunfish (*Lepomis cyanellus*) and bluegill (*Lepomis macrochirus*) in Harkins Branch (% GBYC metric). Williams Branch rated as "excellent" in 2010.

Habitat and Water Quality

All streams were narrow (< 5m) and shallow (<30 cm) on average, typical of small wadeable streams. Carver Branch was the widest stream in all years sampled, and Williams Branch was the shallowest in all years (Table 3). In 2007, all streams were at their widest and deepest, with highest velocity and discharge. Harkins Branch had the largest substrate sizes, consisting of large pebble and small cobble substrate (Wentworth sizes of 15-17), while Carver Branch consisted of small pebble (Wentworth sizes of 12-13) and Williams Branch consisted of small gravel (Wentworth sizes of 9-10) substrate on average.

Fish cover was primarily small woody debris, with each reach having more than 50% of its area covered by this cover type in all years sampled (Carver Branch 61-67%, Williams Branch 66-70%, Harkins Branch 52-64%). Tree root cover was also commonly found at all three streams (Carver Branch 27-39%, Williams Branch 24-47%, Harkins Branch 27-39%) and overhanging vegetation occurred frequently in Williams Branch (47-60%) and Carver Branch (30-39%).

Banks were relatively stable for Carver Branch and Williams Branch, while Harkins Branch showed larger bank angles, less vegetation, and higher banks (Table 4). A large percentage of banks at Carver Branch and Williams Branch had angles less than 60°, vegetation cover greater than 80%, and bank heights less than 1 m. The exception was Carver Branch in 2006 where banks were less stable due to greater bank angles and less vegetation. Banks at both Carver Branch and Williams Branch consisted of silt or sand/gravel substrate. Harkins Branch had a higher percentage of banks with angles greater than 60°, vegetation cover less than 80%, and heights greater than 2 m. However, a small percentage of the banks at Harkins Branch did consist of more stable cobble substrate. In general, banks were relatively stable for streams at GWCA. Measurements of bank stability, particularly bank angle, percent vegetation, and bank substrate, showed large changes among years within a stream reach (Table 4). Considerable changes in bank characteristics would only be expected if flooding or significant alterations in riparian land use occurred; therefore, the variability found in bank measurements at GWCA is likely due to a result of observational sampling methods rather than a true change in bank stability. Further analysis of bank measurement data is warrented to determine the validity of using observational sampling methods to assess bank stability.

Water quality showed more variability among years than among streams (Table 5). Temperatures and specific conductance were highest in 2006 at all reaches, with average temperatures varying by as much as 6.5 $^{\circ}$C at Williams Branch and 4.1 $^{\circ}$C at Harkins Branch, and specific conductance varying by 132 μS/cm at Harkins Branch and 116 μS/cm at Carver Branch. pH was higher in Carver and Williams branches in 2007 with differences in pH of 2.6 and 1.7, respectively. In general, turbidity was low (<10 NTU), on average, at all sites and in all years but highest in 2007 for all sites. Among streams, Carver Branch was less variable in temperature and dissolved oxygen among years, but more variable in turbidity. Williams and Harkins branches were more variable in temperature and dissolved oxygen. However, the higher average turbidity in Carver Branch in 2007 was due to increased turbidity levels during the night hours, possibly due to terrestrial animal activity in the water or along the bank.

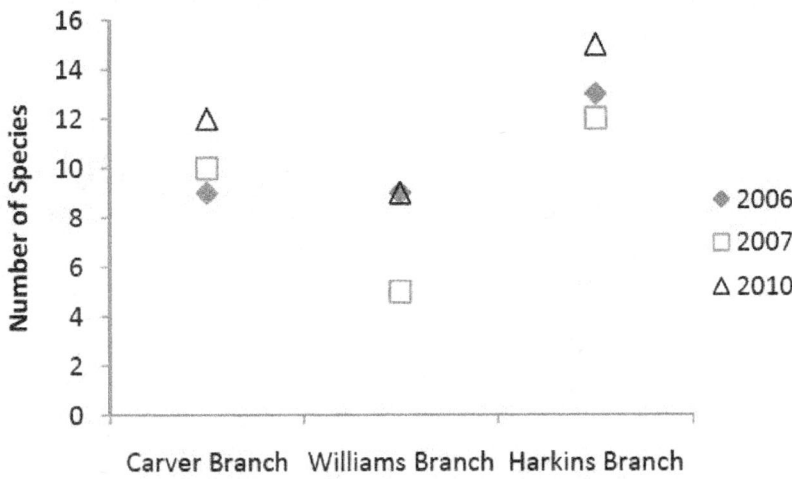

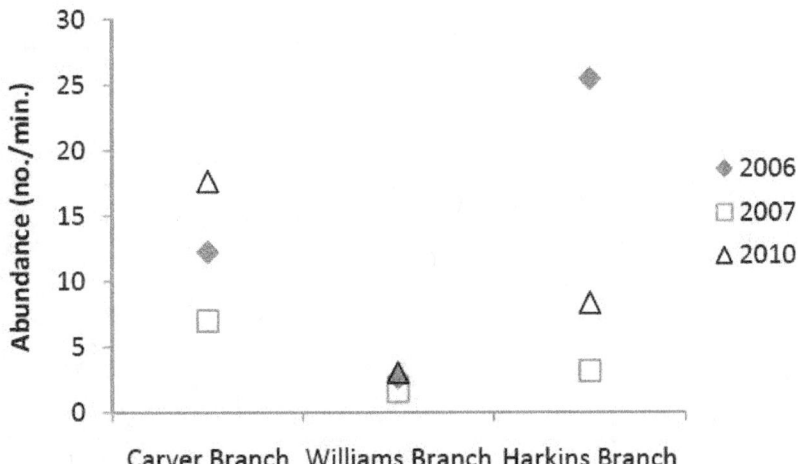

Figure 2. Species richness, community diversity (Simpson's Index), and abundance for reaches sampled at GWCA in 2006, 2007, and 2010.

Table 1. Number of species and percent composition of sucker, sunfish, and sculpin/madtom/darter species for reaches sampled in 2006, 2007, and 2010.

Sample Reach	No. Species Suckers	% Comp Suckers	No. Species Sunfish	% Comp Sunfish	No. Species Darters, Sculpins, Madtoms	% Comp Darters, Sculpins, Madtoms
2006						
Carver Branch	1	0.4	0	0.0	4	13.6
Williams Branch	0	0.0	0	0.0	5	61.9
Harkins Branch	0	0.0	1	0.5	6	10.5
2007						
Carver Branch	1	0.6	1	3.3	5	13.2
Williams Branch	0	0.0	1	4.3	2	87.0
Harkins Branch	0	0.0	2	7.5	6	26.1
2010						
Carver Branch	1	0.5	1	0.8	5	19.8
Williams Branch	0	0.0	0	0.0	6	80.7
Harkins Branch	1	0.3	2	10.7	7	33.1

Table 2. Index of Biotic Integrity (IBI) scores and metric values for each reach sampled in 2006, 2007, and 2010. AHIP = individuals that are Algivorous, Herbivorous, Invertivorous, and Piscivorous, Anom = individuals with an Anomaly (disease, eroded fins, lesions, tumors, or blackspot), GBYC = individuals as Green sunfish, Bluegill, Yellow bullhead, or Channel catfish, Invert = individuals that are invertivorous, Carn = individuals that are top carnivores, DSM = Darter/ Sculpin/Madtom species, Lithophilic = species that are sand/gravel spawners.

Sample Reach	% AHIP	% Anom	% GBYC	% Invert	% Carn	No. DSM Species	No. Lithophilic Species	IBI	IBI Rating
2006									
Carver Branch	0.0	0.0	0.0	15.9	0.0	4	6	63	Good
Williams Branch	0.0	0.0	0.0	66.9	0.0	5	8	80	Good
Harkins Branch	0.0	0.0	0.9	18.0	0.0	6	10	73	Good
2007									
Carver Branch	0.0	0.0	3.3	9.3	0.0	5	9	68	Good
Williams Branch	0.0	0.0	4.3	65.2	0.0	2	4	65	Good
Harkins Branch	1.5	0.0	7.5	17.2	0.0	6	10	67	Good
2010									
Carver Branch	0.0	2.4	0.8	7.3	0.0	5	10	55	Fair
Williams Branch	0.0	0.0	0.0	61.3	0.0	6	9	81	Excellent
Harkins Branch	4.0	15.4	10.7	22.8	0.0	7	13	52	Fair

Table 3. Average width, depth, velocity, and substrate (± one standard error) and total discharge for each reach sampled in 2006, 2007, and 2010.

Sample Reach	Average Width (m)			Average Depth (cm)			Average Velocity (m/s)			Average Substrate (Wentworth Code)			Discharge (m³/s)
2006													
Carver Branch	4.5	±	0.3	17.9	±	2.0	0.02	±	0.00	13.0	±	0.32	0.003
Williams Branch	2.9	±	0.2	4.7	±	0.6	0.07	±	0.01	10.7	±	0.67	0.008
Harkins Branch	3.2	±	0.3	17.9	±	2.0	0.01	±	0.00	17.2	±	0.95	0.003
2007													
Carver Branch	4.8	±	0.4	23.2	±	3.3	0.15	±	0.04	12.7	±	0.62	0.030
Williams Branch	3.5	±	0.2	10.5	±	0.8	0.15	±	0.02	9.8	±	0.77	0.040
Harkins Branch	4.1	±	0.2	28.1	±	2.2	0.23	±	0.04	15.7	±	0.75	0.106
2010													
Carver Branch	4.5	±	0.5	18.0	±	1.9	0.03	±	0.01	12.1	±	0.56	0.009
Williams Branch	3.4	±	0.3	8.2	±	0.7	0.08	±	0.01	8.0	±	0.84	0.014
Harkins Branch	3.4	±	0.5	16.5	±	2.2	0.09	±	0.02	14.6	±	0.76	0.008

Table 4. Bank angle, vegetation, height, and substrate characteristics (in percent of total bank) for each reach sampled in 2006, 2007, and 2010.

	Carver Branch			Williams Branch			Harkins Branch		
	2006	2007	2010	2006	2007	2010	2006	2007	2010
Angle									
< 60°	50	86.4	81.8	81.8	95.5	100	40.9	68.2	63.6
> 60°	50	13.6	18.2	18.2	4.5	0	50.1	31.8	36.4
Vegetation									
>80%	36.4	81.8	100.0	63.6	100.0	100.0	0.0	40.9	59.1
50-80%	63.6	18.2	0.0	36.4	0.0	0.0	81.8	59.1	40.9
<50%	0.0	0.0	0.0	0.0	0.0	0.0	18.2	0.0	0.0
Height									
<1m	72.7	54.5	72.7	100.0	100.0	100.0	50.0	40.9	40.9
1-2m	27.3	40.9	27.3	0.0	0.0	0.0	36.4	27.3	31.8
2-3m	0.0	4.5	0.0	0.0	0.0	0.0	13.6	9.1	27.3
>3m	0.0	0.0	0.0	0.0	0.0	0.0	0.0	22.7	0.0
Substrate									
Silt	81.8	54.5	63.6	100.0	100.0	100.0	36.4	13.6	0.0
Sand/Gravel	18.2	40.9	36.4	0.0	0.0	0.0	63.6	54.5	90.9
Cobble/Boulder	0.0	4.5	0.0	0.0	0.0	0.0	0.0	31.8	9.1

13

Table 5. Average water quality parameters (± one standard error) for each reach sampled in 2006, 2007, and 2010.

Sample Reach	Average Water Temperature (°C)			Average pH			Average Specific Conductance (µS/cm)			Average Dissolved Oxygen (mg/L)			Average Turbidity (NTU)		
2006															
Carver Branch	18.2	±	0.1	7.20	±	0.00	331.5	±	0.1	7.56	±	0.04	1.14	±	0.09
Williams Branch	21.2	±	0.2	7.87	±	0.00	256.6	±	0.2	8.61	±	0.06	4.29	±	0.21
Harkins Branch	20.2	±	0.1	7.22	±	0.01	296.4	±	0.4	5.93	±	0.07	0.74	±	0.04
2007															
Carver Branch	16.0	±	0.2	9.75	±	0.10	215.3	±	3.5	7.58	±	0.17	9.28	±	1.79
Williams Branch	14.7	±	0.1	9.40	±	0.01	178.8	±	0.4	7.89	±	0.05	4.99	±	0.38
Harkins Branch	16.1	±	0.1	6.55	±	0.01	164.3	±	0.3	9.83	±	0.08	5.17	±	0.23
2010															
Carver Branch	15.3	±	0.3	7.39	±	0.00	282.1	±	0.5	7.89	±	0.11	2.19	±	0.30
Williams Branch	17.1	±	0.3	7.75	±	0.00	228.0	±	0.1	10.84	±	0.09	2.95	±	0.77
Harkins Branch	17.3	±	0.3	7.10	±	0.01	214.5	±	0.4	7.34	±	0.19	3.60	±	0.20

Discussion

Fish communities within GWCA are diverse and healthy as evidenced by the numerous species present, high composition of sensitive darter, sculpin, and madtom species, and good IBI score ratings. Harkins Branch typically had higher numbers of species and higher diversity than the other two streams. This stream showed greater bank instability which could lead to bank erosion and sedimentation. However, the fish community remains very diverse, possibly due to the larger substrate and more water (higher discharge) available in Harkins Branch. Although Williams Branch consisted of finer sediments, this stream also had high diversity and the fish community composition consisted predominately of darter, sculpin, and madtom species which usually prefer larger cobble substrates. Carver Branch, which was wider and deeper than the other streams, had relatively high species richness and abundances but lower diversity (i.e., higher Simpson's Index). A high percentage of small woody debris and moderate amounts of tree root cover and overhanging vegetation was present for fish use in these streams, and all reaches showed good stream integrity (i.e., high IBI) and health (low percentage of disease/anomalies), overall. The temporal variation in water quality parameters suggests that annual differences in environmental conditions (rain, temperature, etc.) likely influence water quality in these streams. The lower temporal variability in temperature and dissolved oxygen at Carver Branch could be due to the influence of a spring upstream of the sample reach. In general, streams at GWCA provide good water quality and physical habitat to sustain a diverse native fish community, and provide some protection for the Arkansas darter, a fish species at risk of extirpation throughout its known range.

Literature Cited

Barbour, M. T., J. Gerritsen, B. D. Snyder, and J. B. Stribling. 1999. Rapid bioassessment protocols for use in streams and wadeable rivers: periphyton, benthic macroinvertebrate, and fish, 2nd edition. EPA 841-B-99-002, U.S. Environmental Protection Agency, Washington, DC.

Dauwalter, D. C., E. J. Pert, and W. E. Keith. 2003. An index of biotic integrity for fish assemblages in Ozark Highland Streams of Arkansas. *Southeastern Naturalist* 2:447-468.

Dodd, H. R., D. G. Peitz, G. A. Rowell, D. E. Bowles, and L. M. Morrison. 2008. Protocol for monitoring fish communities in small streams in the Heartland Inventory and Monitoring Network. Natural Resource Report NPS/HTLN/NRR—2008/052. National Park Service, Fort Collins, Colorado.

Karr J. R. 1981. Assessment of biotic integrity using fish communities. *Fisheries* 6:21–27.

Lazorchak, J. M., Klemm, D. J., and D. V. Peck. 1998. Environmental monitoring and assessment program-surface waters: field operations and methods for measuring the ecological condition of wadeable streams. EPA/620/R-94/004F. U.S. Environmental Protection Agency, Washington, DC.

Moulton, S. R. III, J. G. Kennen, R. M. Goldstein, and J. A. Hambrook. 2002. Revised protocols for sampling algal, invertebrate, and fish communities as part of the National Water-Quality Assessment Program. U.S. Geological Survey, Reston, Virginia. Open-file Report 02-150.

National Park Service (NPS). 1999. Resources Management Plan. George Washington Carver National Monument.

Peitz, D.G. 2005. Fish community monitoring in prairie park streams with emphasis on Topeka shiner (*Notropis Topeka*): summary report 2001-2004. National Park Service, Fort Collins, Colorado.

Pflieger, W. L. 1997. The fishes of Missouri. Missouri Department of Conservation, Jefferson City, Missouri.

Robison, H. W., and T. M. Buchanan. 1988. Fishes of Arkansas. University of Arkansas Press, Fayetteville, AR.

Smogor, R. 2005. Draft manual for interpreting Illinois fish IBI scores. Illinois Environmental Protection Agency, Bureau of Water, Surface Water Section

Appendix

Appendix 1. List of species and number collected at GWCA in 2006, 2007, and 2010.

Family	Common Name	Scientific Name	2006	2007	2010
		Carver Branch			
Catostomidae	White sucker	*Catostomus commersoni*	0	2	3
Centrarchidae	Green sunfish	*Lepomis cyanellus*	0	11	5
Cottidae	Banded sculpin	*Cottus carolinae*	0	13	79
Cyprinidae	Cardinal shiner	*Luxilus cardinalis*	1	0	0
Cyprinidae	Creek chub	*Semotilus atromaculatus*	22	10	67
Cyprinidae	Southern redbelly dace	*Phoxinus erythrogaster*	269	247	388
Cyprinidae	Stoneroller spp.	*Campostoma spp.*	0	19	23
Percidae	Arkansas darter	*Etheostoma cragini*	0	1	1
Percidae	Fantail darter	*Etheostoma flabellare*	3	2	0
Percidae	Orangethroat darter	*Etheostoma spectabile*	17	17	3
Percidae	Stippled darter	*Etheostoma punctulatum*	35	11	39
Cyprinidae	Duskystripe Shiner	*Luxilus pilsbryi*	0	0	19
Percidae	Rainbow darter	*Etheostoma caeruleum*	0	0	3
Poeciliidae	Mosquitofish	*Gambusia affinis*	0	0	1
		Williams Branch			
Centrarchidae	Green sunfish	*Lepomis cyanellus*	0	3	0
Cottidae	Banded sculpin	*Cottus carolinae*	8	15	23
Cyprinidae	Creek chub	*Semotilus atromaculatus*	5	1	13
Cyprinidae	Southern redbelly dace	*Phoxinus erythrogaster*	36	5	7
Cyprinidae	Stoneroller spp.	*Campostoma spp.*	3	0	3
Ictaluridae	Slender madtom	*Noturus exilis*	2	0	0
Percidae	Fantail darter	*Etheostoma flabellare*	24	45	49
Percidae	Orangethroat darter	*Etheostoma spectabile*	71	0	7
Percidae	Stippled darter	*Etheostoma punctulatum*	8	0	2
Percidae	Arkansas darter	*Etheostoma cragini*	0	0	9
Percidae	Rainbow darter	*Etheostoma caeruleum*	0	0	6
		Harkins Branch			
Centrarchidae	Bluegill	*Lepomis macrochirus*	0	2	12
Centrarchidae	Green sunfish	*Lepomis cyanellus*	5	8	20
Cottidae	Banded sculpin	*Cottus carolinae*	5	12	31
Cyprinidae	Cardinal shiner	*Luxilus cardinalis*	4	2	0
Cyprinidae	Creek chub	*Semotilus atromaculatus*	32	26	31
Cyprinidae	Non-carp minnow spp.	*Cyprinidae spp.*	12	0	0
Cyprinidae	Southern redbelly dace	*Phoxinus erythrogaster*	79	43	46

Appendix 1. cont.

Family	Common Name	Scientific Name	2006	2007	2010
Cyprinidae	Stoneroller spp.	*Campostoma spp.*	306	18	86
Ictaluridae	Slender madtom	*Noturus exilis*	1	3	0
Percidae	Arkansas darter	*Etheostoma cragini*	6	0	1
Percidae	Fantail darter	*Etheostoma flabellare*	4	7	21
Percidae	Orangethroat darter	*Etheostoma spectabile*	61	4	11
Percidae	Rainbow darter	*Etheostoma caeruleum*	0	1	6
Percidae	Stippled darter	*Etheostoma punctulatum*	26	8	28
Poeciliidae	Mosquitofish	*Gambusia affinis*	3	0	0
Catostomidae	White sucker	*Catostomus commersoni*	0	0	1
Cyprinidae	Duskystripe Shiner	*Luxilus pilsbryi*	0	0	3
Ictaluridae	Stonecat	*Noturus flavus*	0	0	1
Ictaluridae	Black bullhead	*Ameiurus melas*	0	0	1